Mind Spirit

Mapping

A Journey to Purpose

SARAH BREEN

An Earth Lodge® Publication

Wallingford, Vermont, U.S.A

*** This book contains valuable information ***
but it is not intended to take the place of medical care and expertise. Please seek qualified professional care for physical, emotional, and mental health problems.

Mind Spirit
Mapping

Table of Contents

1   Introduction

3   What Happened and Why am I here?

6   Asking the Right Questions

10   Getting to Know Yourself through Purpose

16   Know your Vision and Blueprint

23   Understanding the importance of Decisions

27   What Holds You Back?

31   Spiritual Assets

42   The Map Begins with Thinking

46   Fear and Success

51   Gratitude Simplified

55   Balance

59   Belief and Faith

63   Determining Goals or Focus Points

67   Holding Space for What's to Come

71   The Art of Detachment

76   Remembering and Awakening

78   Separating Mind and Heart

81   The Truth of it All

85   Putting it Together

Introduction

Welcome to Mind Spirit Mapping™.

This is a channeled and designed process that will bring you from a state of confusion to a state of knowing and well-being, to complete oneness with your own unique purpose and mission. It is your job to challenge your own beliefs, while gaining the understanding to move from your current reality to a redesigned reality, one where you call the shots and dance with life as it was designed to be, free from illusions placed on you by others, free to live the life you KNOW is yours to live.

It is our understanding that every belief, theory, religion, scientific study, spiritualism, ancient wisdom, and knowledge has been pointing to a very similar concept, that each person is unique, with her or his own personality traits on the physical plane, that do NOT identify them with their true nature. The true nature of you is something that is felt and cannot be spoken in linguistics. It is a "coming home" feeling, a purpose flowing through you, an energy force one cannot describe, a truth that you can KNOW on a fundamental level.

You will be challenged, as life is like a spiral spinning upward as you evolve with this ever-changing reality. A traditional map shows you the way from points A to Z; the mind spirit map navigates the realms of mind, body, and spirit. You will travel these realms yourself as you watch your map unfold. There are many choices, turns, observations, and transformations that will happen on this journey. Be easy with yourself. Learn how to trust yourself. This process starts here, where you are now. Not where you were five years ago. But right NOW. Drop your expectations to reach the earlier "thinner, spunkier" you! EXPECT to EVOLVE into your true nature, the true ESSENCE of YOU.

Your journey begins NOW.

Chapter 1

What Happened & Why am I here?

𝒴ou may feel like you have lost your way, lost your purpose, lost who you are. Many situations, life experiences, people, and unexpected events occur in our lives that may or may not have been for our best, or so we believe. So, what really happened? You are DISCONNECTED! Unplugged... no power source... your gas light is on... and your battery is flashing red! It took years of events and life experiences, creating beliefs around the idea that it is acceptable to be completely disengaged from who you really are. Been there!

Life just seems to stop flowing and it feels more like walking through quicksand. Panic, anxiety, worry, and fear is a daily knock on the door in your mind. What would happen if ___ happened? What do I do about ____? What am I supposed to do with ___? The list goes on and on. So, what really happened to get you to this point? I began my search for the answers shortly after I decided not to take my own life one cold rainy September day.

Thoughts raced through my head... why am I here? Is this some kind of joke? Is life really just a rat race? What is the purpose of all of this?? I was driving myself mad looking for answers. I found countless books and motivational speakers that would hype me up, only to fall on my face months later. I even dug into ancient philosophy which left me with more questions than answers. But I admit to being someone who enjoys breaking things apart and putting them back together until it makes sense in the easiest way possible. I enjoyed stumping people with rhetorical questions and the never-ending whys until their eyes would roll in the backs of their heads. But... this is one journey that has taken me from high points, to low points, and dancing in between, for a long, long time.

So, what happened to get you here? You willingly followed someone else's bliss. You may have done it consciously or unconsciously, but, either way, you are right here, right now. So, step up to the plate and take a hard look at where you have been. You will immediately think of each situation you perceive has done you or your family wrong. It's ok. You must start somewhere. Now the next step... breathe in... breathe out... and let it go... for now!

You see, every action of energy disbursement has an immediate reaction or ripple effect placed upon it in our realm. The effects of those ripples solely rely on your focus upon it. You got it! Your constant attention to something is causing those ripples to turn into waves. Don't get me wrong, waves are fun until you find the undertow, then you are in a world of trouble in seconds.

This word DISCONNECTED, it feels right, doesn't it? When you look in the mirror you have no idea who is looking back at you, SO, you call yourself your name, your job title, and your college degrees. But it doesn't tell you WHY you're disconnected. You are disconnected because you hold vibrational belief patterns (ripple effects) within you that do NOT match who you are at your core. PERIOD!

I am all about simplicity, and simple is what you will get. You may find it hard to swallow some of the concepts on these pages but my purpose in life is to translate the jargon into easy to understand answers. The box you have been living in your entire life looks like a fragment of energy from afar, a FRAGMENT of what you can be. I am not saying this from an ego standpoint... I am saying this because I love everyone for who they are, where they are, on their evolution to the center of themselves, which ultimately is the core of ALL! This may be hard to believe now but I can assure you the more you are willing to look at yourself, the more you will be able to control your outcomes.

Control?!?!?!? Yes, we love control! That is the main reason why people are so disconnected. Their focus is on controlling the outcome rather than WHAT to control in your daily life. So, yes, you will learn to control your life by finding the center of you first. Why are you here then? To be YOU fully and then EXPAND!

Chapter 2

Asking the Right Questions

$\mathcal{A}$ valuable lesson in this process is learning to ask yourself the right questions. Asking why to every question is great as a child but as an adult, it can make a mountain out of a molehill. We are dedicated to giving you more than enough understanding on the topic of yourself, vibrational placement, and much more, so it will satisfy the "why" child inside of you. First, we must give ourselves permission to uncover who we really are. Now, you might find that statement strange but I can tell you from experience and teachings that people don't know how to give themselves permission. We had to ask to use the bathroom, ask our parents if we could use the car or go out with friends. Should I go on? We filter and navigate life through verbal language instead of allowing ourselves to feel first. So, yes, you do have to go through the process of giving yourself permission to uncover YOU, because up to this point you have needed permission for basically everything in your life.

Next, release the burden of things you cannot control. This allows you to jump off the hamster wheel with the expectation of getting out of the cage at some point. How do you do it? By identifying what you do control, and that is ONLY YOU, not your spouse, child, boss, coworkers, friends, etc. You only control YOU and how you think, feel, and act. If you continually try to control others, you are destined to a lifetime of running on a hamster wheel. You won't get anywhere. Parents may have a different opinion. But mull this over; as a parent myself, the only thing I am responsible for is creating a safe and thriving environment for my children to grow and expand as we are all meant to do. Imagine a world where children grew up encouraged to fully be the core of themselves, day in and day out? They would never feel disconnected or have events in their lives like we have gone through ourselves. HOPE lies in the hands of our future; your job as a parent is to focus on expanding you, and your children will blossom just as fast, if not faster than you could ever imagine.

In any situation in which you dislike the outcome, begin to ask yourself questions like:

What does this mean to me?

What was the prominent feeling in this situation?

What would I want to feel instead?

Notice there are no HOW or WHY questions in there? They all start with WHAT. A what question makes you think about you in the situation. It makes you think deeper to uncover what really matters in the situation. What matters most is how you feel. If you feel miserable more than joyful, this is the greatest indicator of your disconnection. You can't experience your center in a state of misery, like a child having a temper tantrum; your center is a soft nudge, a gentle feeling, that you experience when in a calm state.

Starting today, begin to take responsibility for everything that has happened to you, and everything you are creating. You have created the world around you, both consciously and unconsciously. You may not like hearing it but everything that has happened has served a purpose in your evolving life. It has served its purpose in the evolution of your journey. Taking responsibility for your own thoughts, feelings, actions, and reactions will serve you in learning to listen to the core of you. Your focus should be that which we are all striving for and achieving each day: full enjoyment of the present and ever-expanding abundance. Focus on finding your core truth and invite it in.

Our world is evolving at an unprecedented rate. Not in a bad way, in a good way in terms of mass consciousness. Because of people like you, our future is so much brighter. I believe the reason our species is still here on this planet is because we choose to ask the right questions and, because we always receive an answer, we will continue to evolve faster than ever before. So brace yourself and do not be afraid of uncovering your truth. Do not be afraid as it will meet you like a welcome home surprise party. You are so loved on so many levels, dimensions, and realms. You are never alone on this journey, for those who fight your evolution process are those who will be the final stragglers in the push for dimensional uplifting. Call it what you want, words are only words, but you will understand it as you journey to the center of your core, your spirit, your full truth.

Chapter 3

Getting to Know Yourself through Purpose

If you feel like your life isn't working out, or you're walking in circles, then this is a sign that you are not listening to your core, your heart, or living with purpose.

You may feel numb, overwhelmed, exhausted, or even downright confused when you have a moment to sit with your thoughts.

Without a purpose consciously identified, you will feel like life is happening to you, not for you. We are all on the same path in life.... But what you DO on that path is individual and specific to your purpose. That is what makes us the expanding beings we are.

In fact, it's the largest factor that separates us from animals. We have a reasoning MIND that allows us to CHOOSE what we DO on our path, on our journey to a life full of purpose.

Take a moment to hear this warning: if you do not take the efforts to discover and live your purpose, then much of your life will be spent running in circles, putting out fires, and living this life of struggle that main stream identifies as normal.

But you - yes, you - you had a flame that lit up inside you that told you, "there is something more than what you see today." And you're absolutely right.... Your life has a purpose! That is what we are here to discover.

Now, this isn't something you come to a complete realization of overnight. This is a process of discovery. I challenge you today to take the first steps to uncover your purpose.

Your purpose is your WHY. This is WHO YOU ARE. Your purpose serves as a lifeline you hold to your heart. It helps you form beliefs, decisions, actions, and, ultimately, the results you achieve. So yes, this is a critical piece to the puzzle we call LIFE. You may think this is a difficult task at first so please be gentle with yourself. You can choose to stare at a mountain from afar, or you can choose to walk towards it.

You do not have to accept these ideas but I ask you to not reject them completely either. Understand that we are all creative beings with the abilities to create anything we want in our lives if it matches our core purpose, beliefs, and intentions. That is what you are here to learn and apply to create a well-rounded life, full of everything you can imagine.

We create our lives moment by moment in the creative fields of our mind and heart. But to live the results you want... we must begin by living and leading with your purpose, your heart center.

In your mind, build the foundation that will hold the map for the life you will create from here on out. Discovering your purpose gives you the direction you desire. It's an inner calling that drives all the forces you need to acquire all that you are. There is something in your life that you love doing. Keep thoughts of, "well, I can't see how I can make money doing that," at bay. Those ideas will keep you living the same results over and over.

Fall in love with your center. What is love? It is an energy felt in your heart that can be reflected outside of you in terms of appreciation. This energy equates to a feeling. We want you to fall in love with those things that make you feel alive, excited, fulfilled, appreciative, and whole. When this happens it means that your mind and spirit have reconnected. When you start to find your purpose, IT GUIDES YOU. You begin to see the synchronicities in life – chance meetings and conversations that help you consciously identify your purpose. No control is needed, you need only follow and listen. Any action you think you need to take will be felt through your heart, not your mind.

Acting from the heart is acting with purpose and intention. It sparks your inner child and the possibilities begin to appear. It ignites your imagination. You start acting with PURPOSE, desire, and love. You compose your own symphony when you start living from your heart.

Here is a warning... know that negative ideas and experiences have been bombarding our existence since the day we were born. From trying to fit in, to red marks on tests, you have a conscious awareness of all the negativity and failures in life. That is exactly what has shut your heart down and keeps you from listening to it. Let's face it, the masses are afraid of change so they decide to conform instead. They would rather keep things the same than express the unique, creative abilities of each individual. You must acknowledge the uniqueness you hold inside yourself.

When you focus on the mysteries of yourself, you will ignite the flames of opportunity. The spaces open up in your mind and spirit to align with opportunities you otherwise would have missed before. You begin to see the shifting around you and your thoughts. Things begin to show up to amplify who you really are. Like attracts like... therefore you will attract what is dominant in your mind and then what is in your spirit. Make sure you are asking yourself the right questions.

Purpose gives meaning to WHY you are doing what you're doing. You don't need to justify it to anyone else. It's time to listen to that inner voice. That is what this is all about! Your inner voice will never steer you wrong! You must give serious attention to what comes naturally to you. We think our paths in life should be hard instead of allowing our natural gifts to shine through. We take for granted what comes naturally to us without acknowledging that it's our hearts guiding us. Mull that over for a minute and feel a different force awaken within you.

You are NOT on this planet to live someone else's dream but to create your own! Walking a path not consciously designed by you will never bring you happiness because it was never yours to begin with. Determining your purpose is an internal process of taking responsibility for reconnecting to your heart; you cannot expect your family and friends to answer questions only your heart knows the answers to. Resentment is born from situations like that. When you believe you have found your purpose...DO NOT allow yourself to be persuaded differently by others. Do not allow them to tell you how you should build or in which direction. I suggest keeping it to yourself and allow your imagination to take the lead. Start by asking yourself the right questions to uncover the mysteries inside of you, the things that make you tick.

Here are some questions to ask yourself:

- What accomplishments have you achieved?

- What makes you different from others?

- What creative ideas repeat often in your mind?

- What characteristics do you hold inside of you?

- What comes naturally to you?

- What sparks your interest?

- What do you value the most?

- What do you love to do in your free time?

- What activities do you participate in that seem to make you lose track of time?

•What experiences have given you the opportunity to grow?

Notice that when you are answering some of these questions that they are mostly, if not all, creatively based. These questions are simple but will take some time to digest. We as humans overcomplicate everything in our lives because we must know the answers to everything. Don't compare yourself to others. Every heart is unique and beats to its' own drum. If you find yourself focusing on others, take some deep breaths and refocus your thoughts on all the good that is inside you.

Life is simple and creative! You can either accept that idea or reject it. Either way, your results will show it.

This is your starting point. You must know where you are on the map in order to get where you want to be. Take a moment and breathe. Note that all that has been presented in your life has prepared you for this moment. For this is a new day, new opportunity, a pushpin on a map with a string to your next destination. This is a journey of life fulfillment in ALL areas of your life. Consider the above questions carefully as they are the key to unlocking your heart on this journey.

Chapter 4

Know Your Vision and Blueprint

Now that we know where you are.... It's time to make a conscious choice about where you want to go. Most people, when asked what they want in life, will give you answers such as "I want a million dollars!" or "I just want to be free!". These answers are great and not something to disregard. But if you sit with the simple question of, "What do you want?" your head may begin to spin or you may not even know where to begin.

Place this idea in the back of your mind as you continue with this process... understand that nothing is ever permanent, and everything is always changing. With that in the back of your mind, now let's gain a greater understanding of visioneering and the importance it has upon your life.

As a small child, you had a natural understanding of this idea called imagination. Clouds turned into your playhouse and the grass you laid upon became your audience. Your mind is the most impressive tool you can utilize to regain your cellular memory of imagination. In fact, without the use of your imagination your life would not be what it is today, good, bad, or indifferent. Think of this: if you have ever said to yourself, "I knew that would turn out like that," you used your imagination to create that reality.

Now, I may have struck a chord, so I'll say it again. You utilize your imagination each day to create your reality, moment by moment. Life is an illusion that is created in your mind. If life hasn't gone the way you planned it to be, then it's ok to admit that you have been imagining in the "I don't want that to happen" direction.

Consciously understanding yourself, mind, body, and spirit, will lead you to develop your thoughts, feelings, and responses in an enlightened manner, thus leading you to the wholeness that is uniquely you.

Let's turn your attention to desire. Desire begins with a vision, a vision is coupled with purpose, and your purpose is the guiding force in your life. Your desires are unique and can be anything from feelings to material possessions. But know that every desire will equal out to a feeling which links to your core values. The key behind creating your vision is to give yourself permission to think wild and free. To not put the, "yeah, buts," or, "how am I going to do this?" or, "Let's be realistic," into this. Go wild and make a decision to begin this process of thinking outside of the box.

Once you begin the imagination process, the vision itself needs to be flexible. We live in a yes or no world with no gray possibilities. We are programmed that flexibility means chaos and no structure. As you walk this journey and really dive into the nuts and bolts of who you are, you will begin to pick up pieces of yourself that have been missing for a very long time. That, in itself, is a very freeing feeling.

I am not here to tell you what your vision is; I am here to guide and prod your mind to reunite with the essence, the spirit, of you. Words never teach, your experiences do. Therefore, it is your job to exercise your mind to reconnect yourself back to your TRUTH. I state this with confidence because this is how this process has been exercised for centuries starting with the indigenous people of our time. Back then, they had silence, solitude, and life without a clock. Today we have nothing but noise and social media, and time feels like it's running out day in and day out. It is your time now to regain your balance and walk the path that calls to you every moment of every day.

Exercising your imagination is a gentle process, one that requires you to not set demands or timeframes that create stress and force. Begin when your state of mind is at ease and relaxed. Carve out time for yourself to create a space to relax and allow your mind to explore your desires. This is the process of rediscovering who you really are. In doing so, you recommit to the promises you made to yourself and will release thoughts of unworthiness, those feelings that broke your spirit time and again.

You may begin by identifying your needs. As you write down your needs, pay special attention to where they are coming from. Are they coming from lack and limitation or are they coming from a deep loving desire from within? You will begin to feel the difference as you continue to write. Your needs will turn into your wants, and your wants into a vision. One last step in this process is staying true to your values. By identifying your core values, you begin to see patterns in your desires and visions. Are they in alignment with your own truth? If we operate outside of our core values, no matter how much energy you put into something, it will never turn out the way you want it to be. Theology states rejection is God's protection.

Identifying your core values is not a step you want to skip. It helps you identify what is most important to you and what uniquely drives you; it grounds and aligns you with who you really are and helps you understand how and why you tick.

It's time to step into your vision. It's time to walk the path that you create. It's time to live by your own design because that is the journey we live to experience.

Core Values Exercise

Step 1: Brainstorm Your Key Values

Start with taking the list below and quickly circle the words that jump out at you. Do not overthink this process as we need to have your gut tell us what is most important to you. These words help you feel something at your core. Simply circle as many words as you feel needed. This is a general list and you may add any words to it that you feel are personally important to you.

Abundance	Accountability	Acceptance
Awareness	Achievement	Advancement
Ambition	Accomplishment	Adventure
Affection	Appreciation	Balance
Beauty	Boldness	Brilliance
Calmness	Caring	Challenge
Community	Commitment	Charity
Compassion	Confidence	Connection
Collaboration	Consciousness	Contribution
Creativity	Curiosity	Courage
Credibility	Consistency	Courtesy
Dedication	Daring	Dependability
Determination	Dignity	Discovery
Discipline	Decisiveness	Drive
Empathy	Effectiveness	Energy
Enthusiasm	Enjoyment	Ethical
Excellence	Expressiveness	Experience
Family	Fairness	Fearless
Flexibility	Focus	Freedom
Fun	Friendship	Giving
Generosity	Grace	Gratitude
Growth	Happiness	Hard Work

Health	Honesty	Humor
Humility	Harmony	Intimacy
Integrity	Intuitive	Intelligence
Inspiring	Justice	Joy
Kindness	Knowledge	Love
Learning	Leadership	Loyalty
Liberty	Logic	Making a Difference
Mindfulness	Moderation	Motivation
Mastery	Meaning	Openness
Order	Optimism	Originality
Organization	Open-Minded	Passion
Peace	Performance	Personal Development
Prosperity	Purpose	Professionalism
Quality	Reason	Recognition
Respect	Reflective	Reliability
Resourcefulness	Responsibility	Risk
Resilient	Service	Sharing
Spirituality	Simplicity	Security
Silence	Skillfulness	Stability
Serenity	Sensitivity	Structure
Success	Support	Talent
Teamwork	Thoughtfulness	Trustworthiness
Tranquility	Truth	Traditional

Uniqueness	Usefulness	Understanding
Unity	Vision	Victory
Valor	Versatility	Well-Being
Warmth	Wealth	Wisdom

Step 2: Group Your Values

Next, take your list of circled words and begin to group similar words together into categories. Create up to five main groups. Base your grouping solely on what makes the most sense to you.

Step 3: Identify Your Groups

Choose one value from each group that you feel best describes that entire section and use that to label your group. Please do not overthink or analyze this part. When reaching for this value you will create all that is explained within that group. Each value describes the meaning of your main choice in each section. Have fun with this!

Chapter 5

Understanding the Importance of Decisions

"*Decisions*, decisions, decisions..." This phrase always leads to someone not making a decision. Just the idea of making the decision puts your mind in a loop. *"What do you want to eat?" "I don't know, what do you feel like?"* We can all identify with this conversation, having experienced it many times.

Decision making is a basic but imperative skill to reteach yourself. You heard that correctly - reteach yourself how to make decisions. You make decisions all day long in business, family, and social settings, but when it comes to making a decision that will put you in alignment with who you really are, you may find yourself with more questions than answers, making it difficult to reach a resolution.

What is the meaning of the word decision? According to the dictionary, it is "a conclusion or resolution after consideration," yet many people suffer from procrastination, which by definition, is "the action of delaying or postponing something."

So after careful consideration, we have concluded that the cure to procrastination is – let's hear it - DECISION! You may smirk at these simple definitions but the conscious repetition of hearing the simplicity of it will help you more than you realize. When you neglect to make an evolving decision, you are carving deeper grooves into your mind that keep you in a rut: same actions create the same results. It's like pressing play on a familiar song and expecting to hear something different.

The next question we hear so often is, "How do I know I am making the right decision?" This is a very important question when you are starting out because we have made many decisions in the past that may or may not have created the results you intended.

This now brings us to what this entire journey is all about. It's about learning to make evolutionary decisions by listening to the inner voice, your intuition, that has been there since you were a child. It is my goal to give you the tools you need to become who you intended at birth. Through all the experiences in my life, I have embraced the idea that I thought differently than others. I would pick a situation up and look at all angles, all sides, and way beyond the box to seek what felt right. I had the privilege as a child to have a mother who encouraged me to embrace my individuality and experience life the way I creatively saw fit. Of course, my mother created the safest space possible for me to do so, and those moments growing up making decisions by following my feelings is what led me to be able to guide you through what really works.

Your decisions must come from the core of you. As you walk along this process there is a key question you must ask yourself; this question is, "Is this a step towards my desire?" In other words, "Does it feel good to go this way, or does it feel uncomfortable and lead me away from my desire?" Then, you must listen to the first response your core tells you. It is usually a quick yes or no but sometimes you get a pause or maybe nothing. Often, a core response will present as an expansion or opening in your heart area (yes!) or a constriction of the upper torso where your shoulders hunch forward and a weight settles into your chest (no!) Sometimes, a yes will feel like pure joy and excitement, while a no might make your stomach clench or feel nauseous. All these responses are normal while you learn to take the cues from your core. Pay attention to the first response only; anything beyond that will make you overthink, leading to doubt, resentment, guilt, or fear. If the pause happens, put the question aside and come back to it within twenty-four hours.

The point of this simple question is to help you gain the confidence that you hold the answer inside. Ultimately, you're reigniting the belief you had inside yourself all along. We live in an action-oriented world; we think nothing will get done unless we do it ourselves, and we have forgotten how to pause and move from our core. Living in a very busy, noisy world, there is a gap in modern day personal growth. That gap is holding a space for the most powerful part of you to fly. Many self-help books and spiritualties talk about an invisible force that operates the larger part of you. Most people can agree that we are a shell that embodies an energy to experience this life on a spiritual and physical level together.

So, what does this have to do with decisions? Decide today to explore that largest part of you, to use that creative side of you in a constructive and humble manner in order to obtain a life of well-being in terms of balance, harmony, and happiness in every area of your life. The remaining part of you is your free will. You have the ability to choose to embrace it or numb it more. I'm choosing right now to create balance and harmony through centering my higher self, giving you the tools to assist you, and watching you fly. It's your decision. Will you choose to take the leap?

Chapter 6

What Holds You Back?

So far, we have talked about your purpose, the process of reigniting your imagination, and what the decision-making process should look like. Now it is time to talk about the purple elephant in the room: the blocks!

You may or may not have heard the term paradigm. For our purposes, a paradigm can be defined as a pattern of thought that keeps repeating in your mind; it ultimately turns into a belief that may or may not be true to the core of you. For all intents and purposes, a paradigm is a belief you have in your mind that shapes your results and the reality you experience.

How do you release the blocks, those stepping stones that lead to less than satisfactory results? Change the paradigm or belief about the idea and your results will change with it. That's easier said than done because you have an entire lifetime of experiences that have created your belief or judgment about a situation.

To break through these blocks, we must always remain curious. Every thought, reaction, and conclusion we have in our lives is created by a dominant thought pattern in our minds. To remain curious is to begin to use the simple question we have talked about in the previous section, "Is this a step towards my desire or does it lead me away from it?"

By beginning this process of questioning your beliefs, how things should work out, or why you do the things you do when you know you should be doing something else, you will find a pattern in your thinking. Your job is to find a common thread throughout these thoughts. Could this be coming from an idea of lack, feeling unworthy, or just plain fear? The threads might connect back to intricately knit ideas. Notice how those threads are completely opposite to what you value the most in your life. Notice how you feel when you speak out loud to yourself. Now, notice how these threads weave through your experiences and affect the pattern every time you approach something new.

With enough understanding of a paradigm, you can begin to challenge those ideas and conclude the truth about them. This isn't a small task by any means and is completely part of your journey day in and day out. Each experience, situation, and chance meeting will give you the unique opportunity to uncover those patterns and create a new pattern moving forward. What we are really talking about here is a practice of centering your emotions and then moving them in a direction that matters the most to you; your core. Your paradigms create your habits. You may have a habit of reacting a certain way about relationships, money, your job, or even other people's success. Identifying your core values will create the map leading to your true core.

Your blocks are your conditioned way of thinking on autopilot. Until you become conscious of your automatic choices and reactions, your results will never change. Taking this one step further, where your focus goes (consciously or unconsciously) your results will always show.

How do you change your results?

By working on the creative side of you - your spiritual assets, the side of you that has been buried and locked in a box. You know the box is there, but did you know you hold the key to unlock it? Through the process of Mind Spirit Mapping™, you will unlock your spiritual assets and operate with a full understanding of how the game of life works. On a side note, please understand that you are programmed to think in sequential processes. But each individual person has his or her own process or spiral in life that is unique to his or her own unfoldment. You will begin to see the purpose of all this when you are willing and open to your own journey.

Starting today, remain aware of your results to date. This is not a time to hash up old memories or place blame. This is a time to slow the freight train down by asking yourself, "What did that mean to me?" Slowly, one by one, each rock-hard, stubborn block will begin to soften, and you will anchor your emotions to a neutral point where you can do some core work.

Before you move on and work with your spiritual assets, be aware of where your paradigms show their ugly faces. Begin by pondering this question:

In what ways do you feel life has been unfair?

This will give you a starting point. Remain curious and realize that your emotions can easily cloud your judgment if you allow them to. The more you practice remaining open and neutral, the easier it will become to dictate the outcome of that emotional focal point.

Answering the question will create fertile ground into which you can plant seeds. When a seed starts to sprout, the dirt comes up with it as it reaches towards the sun, but the goal is continual positive growth. The dirt, or paradigms, must come up! This means, if you're willing to face your decisions in a centered manner, you can focus on your journey. That is the true nature of manifestation.

Chapter 7

Spiritual Assets

We will break spiritual assets down into creative tools. You can master any situation once you learn how to utilize them. They are as follows: Reason, Will, Memory and Perception, which are located in your mind, and, Imagination and Intuition, which are located within your spirit. These are the tools you were born with, utilized as a child, and then slowly repressed as you were pressured to conform.

As a child, your world revolved around you. Your days were spent engaging in play, fun, and joy. Granted, not every moment was pure joy for everyone, but those feelings of complete enjoyment and appreciation were far more powerful than negative thoughts placed upon you by others. You heard that correctly: negative thoughts – other people's paradigms - were placed in your mind in attempts to save you from getting hurt or doing something that didn't fit communal standards of behavior. This was usually done in your best interest according to someone else's idea of boundaries. But something inside of you knew that it really wasn't true to your core.

I was a natural challenger. I think my mother turned gray the moment I took my first steps. Challenging was my job and I continue to do so each day. This is how I grow. Now, I don't mean challenge in terms of picking a fight, I mean questioning everything in a curious but independent manner. Once I reawakened my spiritual assets as an adult, I realized very quickly that what I felt inside all along was my truth. I was finally coming home. It was my core speaking to me softly. And guess what - it felt amazing to recognize those soft nudges and follow them without fear or doubt. I am giving you a glimpse of your future, a future where you call the shots and watch your life blossom. Now, this is all done with your spiritual assets, your highest intentions for good, and a burning desire and knowing that your joy and happiness is your top priority!

The question we always hear is, "Am I being selfish by focusing on my own happiness?" I encourage you to experiment to find your answer. Ask yourself that question again and realize how we are programmed to put others' needs above our own. A common analogy is the safety instructions given before taking off on a flight: "Always remember to put the oxygen mask on yourself first before helping others." How can you help others with their masks if you can't breathe? Next time you think it's selfish to focus on your own emotions and happiness, see what it does to the people around you as they watch you relive the same results again and again, not following your core. As you proceed through this journey, you will begin to see that, by working on your own patterns of thought, it will clear or ripple into past, present, and future generational lines. By working on yourself, you can ripple your energy through generations with one change in your pattern, one break of a cycle, one glimpse into your core truth. People around may not know what you're doing but they can feel it on a level that cannot be spoken. You may not fully accept the idea at this moment, so play with it briefly and then let it go.

Reason

Let's talk about the first spiritual asset: your ability to reason. Reason is, by definition, "the action of thinking about something in a logical, sensible way." My question, then, is what is a logical way? In fact, the definition of logical is, "natural or sensible given the circumstances." Things that seem sensible or logical are just ideas that were pondered until an agreement was made. Therefore, your ability to reason is based solely upon your beliefs and experiences. What is normal? What is logical? You create your own logic, your own normal, your own beliefs, but no one ever told you that you have the ability or permission to do so. Now understand that each person, culture, business, and society has its own values which in turn create their own logical beliefs, and, therefore, reasoning abilities. Each person, culture, business, and society has created its own set of rules that coincide with their values. This is what creates their sense of logic and ability to reason or think outside the box. That is why people or businesses get upset when their values are violated.

Reason gives you permission to assert if something is within your best interest. Asking yourself if this idea will help or hurt you will rest solely on your logical thinking and beliefs. If you are pondering whether or not something is in your best interest, then you call upon your other spiritual assets to determine the best answer for you.

Children perceive new situations from a fresh, innocent point of view. They NATURALLY understand that this world is a wonderous playground, one in which they can create what they want and do what they want with it, all for the purpose of JOY. Your job is not to crush their reasoning ability but to learn from it. Keep them safe without instilling fear in their minds. Teach them how to be a human but don't break their spirits through your paradigms and "logic".

My oldest child can reason his way through any situation and embrace his true core. I facilitate his way of thinking, allowing him to bloom into a beacon of pure love and joy. Most of us need to reset our ability to reason, and observing children will help you reach your innermost child.

Will

The definition of will is, "a deliberate or fixed desire or intention." This is your ACTION spiritual asset. It is one you will want to make a part of your core. Your will is your ability to focus. For some, the ability to focus is an easy task, while others find it daunting. For example, some people thrive off of sitting quietly in a meditative state while others cannot shut their minds off long enough to do so. Both of these feelings are perfectly normal. Understand that it takes practice to strengthen your will, making it easier to connect with your spiritual assets.

Please don't confuse will with willpower. When we look at the word will, we tend to think in terms of willpower. This isn't an exercise of forcing yourself to avoid doing something based on a goal as it is a new way of being. Your will is your ABILITY to take your reasoned choice and HOLD it in your mind until it integrates with your heart. No force is necessary as using force can be counterproductive to your core.

Your will helps you focus on what really matters to you. It holds your truth on your journey and helps you separate what is truly you from outside ideas. Your will helps you choose your heart over your ego, helps you feel the spaces between objects to reveal their true nature, and is a knowing that guides you to HOLD that feeling, thought, or image in your heart. It helps you come home!

Memory

Memory! "I have a terrible memory!" is a common phrase we hear on a regularly. This cannot be further from the truth. Unfortunately, we associate memory with the memorizing we learned in school instead of the amazing spiritual asset we can call upon. Memorizing is knowledge-based mental storage. We are asked to memorize school work or directions to and from a destination.

Memory can be defined as, "the faculty by which the mind stores and remembers information." The keyword in that definition is mind. How is the mind separate from your brain? Let's simplify this; your mind is an energy force that runs through every cell of your being while your brain is an organ that keeps the physical body alive. You do not think about breathing, you just breathe. You do not think about blinking, you just blink. That is the job of the brain, a series of cells and nerves that operate like a highway of communication that keep you out of physical danger. Now comes another question: do the mind and brain both have memory? YES, they do. Your brain has conditioned memory. This means that as a child you may have brushed up against something hot and your nervous system screamed, "HOT! BACK AWAY!". This created a conditioned memory or cellular response that tells your brain an increase in temperature may cause pain and damage to your body. Your brain stores millions of conditioned cellular responses that keep you alive and breathing.

Your mind, on the other hand, is something that flows between the energy spaces of your body and beyond. These spaces hold valuable information that you may not have been aware of. Within this energy, you hold knowledge or data from past lives, ancestral lines, and conditioned responses that have no previous experience within this current lifetime. We hold imprints of energy experiences that are linked to you personally through the consciousness of your energy field. Your mind, when connected back to your spirit, will reveal the truth of your core. Everyone has a perfect spiritual memory that needs to be tapped into to help you evolve on your journey.

You can read this and decide to disregard it. That is completely ok as we are all on this journey together. Know that your memory goes far beyond just remembering your name and address. It goes deeper as you walk through your evolution into reconnecting your mind and spirit as it was always meant to be. Some call it God, the Askash, Ether, Source, Universe, Angels, or Guides to name a few. But know that whatever "language" you choose to use, it is exactly the way you need to digest this idea. Do not get hung up on words as words are only used to describe a feeling. We love you no matter what words you use to describe the memory you hold within your field of being.

Perception

It is in perfect alignment to talk about the next spiritual asset of Perception. Perception is your ability to look at things multi-dimensionally and form insight you otherwise would have overlooked through your conventional program of logical thinking. It can be defined as *"the state of being or process of becoming aware of something through the senses."* Conventionally, you would perceive something through your physical senses; see, hear, smell, taste, touch; and not your energetic senses. Your energetic senses are what we are talking about now with your spiritual assets. Each asset goes hand in hand with your evolution up the spiral of life. What would you do in someone else's physical shoes? How would you know how their life experiences would dictate how they would respond in any situation? You don't unless you exercise your perception within the energetic field.

Taking perception a step further will give you a glimpse into what we are propelling you forward into. Utilizing perception only within a neutral state of being will grant you access into a heart-centered motion of compassion and understanding on a multi-dimensional level. What are dimensional levels? Each aspect of your mind, body, and spirit has an energetic dimension. The number and explanation of dimensional levels is argued among the scientific and spiritual worlds. But in any case, know that there are more levels of dimension than we need to be aware of at this point in our lives. We live in a 3rd dimension of the physical world where our physical senses are utilized to perceive our world. The 4th and 5th dimensions, for our purposes, will be identified as the entrance of the spirit realm; from ego to the heart.

In any case, you are here to seek what matters the most to you, what you perceive as a fulfilling life. We tend to have more of a perception problem than a lack of skills problem. Your perception has created a belief system in you that tells you what you can and cannot do. Have you ever had someone tell you that "you have so much potential locked up inside of you"? It's enough for you to want to punch them square in the face because they tend to not tell you what they see! I've been there! Some of it has been dictated to you till you perceived it as your own truth, and some of it has been a slow resistance to what is true to you; a running away from what feels right to you.

How do we exercise your perception? It's very simple... you STOP and think for a moment. Then you choose (using your ability to reason) to RESPOND in a manner that does not come from your ego; it comes from the heart (using your energetic memory in the spaces). As Epictetus, a Greek philosopher said: *"you have two ears and one mouth, use them in that proportion."*

Imagination

Our imagination is one of the most underutilized spiritual assets in today's society. It is one that gets pushed to the side while we allow the distractions of our outside world to run our minds without skipping a beat. Over time our imagination grows weak, eventually only being used to think about lack and limitation.

As a child, your mind ran wild with the clouds as it turned into animals prancing across the sky. Every box became a spaceship riding up to the moon for the day's exploration. Then suddenly, you were asked to sit still, pay attention, and stop looking out the windows. The imagination grew weary. This is the part of our spirit that shows us, in pictures, what we feel. Conditions of your past dictate your emotional association to an image. Your imagination can run wild to surround you with a beautiful scene or it can create more of the prison you believe you live in. Imagination is the asset of movie-making, it is the creative side of you that can create and move things into form just by grabbing ahold of the idea. Everything that has been created in the world has been created in the mind long before physical form. The idea was sparked from a desire or curiosity to improve; to help a community, a tribe, or your family. Imagination is a form of expansion, and expansion is what we must do.

The beautiful thing about imagination is that it can be utilized in each spiritual asset. If I said "picture a rose petal"... you will notice an experience matched with a feeling come onto the screen of your mind. This is where all of your spiritual assets are being utilized at once. Your memory recalls an event, your will then holds the image in your mind, your imagination plays out scenarios within seconds, your perception then picks apart each scenario, and then the final piece comes into play; your intuition, to tell you what is true to you. Your truth is then tested when you enter the ego in a manner that may or may not be for the growth and expansion of love, that will determine if anything created from that will or will not last.

Intuition

Intuition is defined as *"the ability to understand something immediately, without the need for conscious reasoning."* In other words, it is getting in tune with your gut feelings. Understanding and applying the basic ideas of your spiritual assets will help you strengthen your inner world so it shifts your outer world. Your intuition is a complete knowing without the need to justify why you are doing it. It's an inner guidance, or is it really? The intuition is the highest asset one strives to have the strongest connection with. Why you may ask? Because it links you up to the infinite, the universal consciousness, source, guides, etc. If you break down the word it would read in-tuition. Tuition means to teach or instruct. Then we can hypothesize that intuition means to take instructions or guidance from within.

Once you have a handle on how your intuition presents itself, you will be able to consciously align with that inner guidance. This is what most want to strive for. To know and hold your faith in this direction you are pointed in. The intuition does not stop and explain anything, it just points the way and you must hold the faith to follow it. For example, when you are driving home and out of nowhere you desire to take a different route home, only to find out later that night there was an accident that you would have been involved in if you didn't listen to your intuition. Learn to acknowledge the mysteries of your intuition. Be humble to its place in your life, as it is here to connect you to all that is, all that has been, and all that will be. It is the universe nudging you to your center.

Chapter 8

The Map Begins with Thinking

Now that we have laid the foundation of your spiritual assets, we need to begin with an image of your map. The traditional mind mapping takes an idea and you create branches off of it to organize your thoughts. Here we do things a bit different. We are mapping through your mind to find the spark of your spirit and let the flame do the rest. This is your own unique road map on your own personal journey in your evolution through this lifetime. We have evolved so quickly in a short amount of time due to technology. Now, if we use it correctly you can indeed have a quantum leap in your lifetime. Here is the best part, by you working on yourself... you are benefiting mass consciousness, immediate family, past, present, and future lifetimes. How? Well, that is for you find out – and you will rather quickly. The mysteries of this specific universe are so profound that if we started off telling you how it would benefit everyone, you would get an immediate headache as our minds are not equipped with the capacity to understand existence without time. It is your job to focus only on YOU as we move through this process. It will ripple out exactly where it needs to go to benefit all.

The road map begins with an image we must understand; our mind. Mind is in every cell of your physical body and beyond. It is one with all and all within one. As humans, we have free will. This free will we have been granted two parts of our mind, conscious and unconscious.

Conscious Mind

The conscious mind is where our ability to reason, imagine, and hold intention resides. Our physical senses are also picked up by the conscious mind: see, hear, smell, taste, touch. Why is it when someone loses a physical sense their energy senses are amplified? That is because our physical senses only tell us what is in the physical reality right here right now; the illusion. When one loses their sense of sight, their unconscious sight is awakened... the ability to see through their spiritual sight. We develop our own logic in the conscious mind and when it is in alignment with our center, we operate from that as our truth. Here is where we choose our story. Here is where we take the data from our unconscious mind and make a map between the two in coming home to our truth. Yes, it is our logical mind, but as we stated before, know what you value consciously and link it to your heart.

Unconscious Mind

The unconscious mind is where our intuition and memory reside. It's where some believe the soft nudges come from. For all intents and purposes, you can look at your unconscious mind as being connected to all that was, will be, and is. Some say it's the mass consciousness or universal mind. In any case, your ability to use your intuition is to get your conscious and unconscious mind to align themselves long enough so you can create a new pattern of thought or belief.

There is a great power behind our thoughts. To see the power in the thought ask yourself these questions: Where did the idea or thought come from? Why am I playing with this idea? Is this a good idea? So many of these questions put you in a position to work with your spiritual assets. Your thinking is 100% independent from your current reality. Take a moment to read that line again. Meaning what is happening to you right now just is. It has been created from past decisions (consciously or unconsciously made), actions to counteract reactions, and so on. You are the cause and the now is the effect. IT JUST IS... now leave it be! Stop focusing so much on what is right in front of you and start walking within your core. We want you just for a brief moment to envision a highway between your minds, core self, and your spirit. If you know that your core and spirit is that of only pure love and joy, then what do you think is the issue here? The MIND! You can learn everything about the mind and still at the end of the day... need to throw it all out! Because in the end, all you need is to know is on a heart level what you value, what you love, what brings you joy, and your unconscious mind will begin to reflect more of that. You can learn and devour all the knowledge you want... but in the end, KNOW THYSELF through how you feel and operate within an open mind and heart.

At this point now, we need to take responsibility for the blocked highway we have created in ourselves. Be 100% OK with this. Be still and open. Find what works for you to help you be more open. Taking responsibility does NOT mean it's all your fault that so and so did this or that to you. We cannot control anyone else's decisions, behaviors, or reactions, besides our own. Do not spend any time wondering why things happened the way they did or how it could be different. You may or may not have seen or felt the massive detour signs or roadblocks between your mind and your core spirit. Just with your intention alone to unblock the highway will yield you the experiences that will SHOW you an open highway. You do NOT need to DO anything at the moment. Just hold a space of intent that this shall be done and be open to what's to come. Intention is more powerful to the unconscious and spirit than physical action. JUST BE!

Chapter 9

Fear and Success

Fear has plagued us for GENERATIONS. It was created by man and we refer to fear as a man-made emotion. In fact, if you enjoy history you can go back over time and notice that each and every war was started over fear of losing power.

The phrase *holding the power* is funny to us. Everyone holds the same amount of power, but some channel power in a healing way, while some channel it and use it to create good. Then there are some that do not channel any power but try to take it from others. TRY to take it. We can feel physically tired, but the power never runs out. We can allow fear to create more realities that are never true to your core, or you can allow them to be what they are and not give them a second thought. Remember you can only control YOU and your highway inside yourself and beyond. If you always ask yourself the right questions, fear will begin to fade away. You will focus on you and your relationship to your innermost truth. Fear is from the ego. The ego is not connected to who you really are. Your ego tries to push ideas, beliefs, and conditions onto others. Are you plagued with someone else's insecurity or loss? When you get hit with the ego, love is very far off from it. Only shifting your focus to love and joy will remove fear from thoughts in your mind. Know what you can control and what is your truth in the situation.

What is really going on in your mind and spirit is a battle of vibrations or frequencies that do not match. In your mind, you have created a fear response to an idea that you have no control over, often because it involves other people or agencies who act independently of your desires. Your core or spirit is now disconnected because it only vibrates love and joy, it will not join you in lower vibrations. It now becomes a battle of the mind. Your conscious mind has created fear based upon a single idea. Your unconscious mind is filled with experiences that only equal out to feeling vibrations. The unconscious mind then recalls to the conscious mind a matching feeling vibration, then the conscious mind paints the experience from the feeling vibration; thus, equaling out a relivable fear before you took your next breath. More like lighting striking between both the conscious and unconscious mind but you are neglecting the core of you during the process. We call this being head-focused and not heart-focused.

How do we become heart focused?

Let's turn fear into an experiment. Most fears are around the topics of needing or desiring things to be a certain way; controlling a situation unconsciously. We have become a species of overthinking to the point of complete fear of an uncontrolled outcome; the unknown. Imagination is a wonderful tool to use in the right direction. *"What is the worst thing that could happen?"* is the worst question you can ask an over-thinker with an active imagination. Instead, realize everything doesn't need to be perfect and see that everything that occurs is for your highest and best, based on where you stand right now. Love where you are right now and give yourself permission to give yourself a break! Your fear has been created to please others and never yourself. To please your core, you must stay true to it. Remaining in love and a joyful state of being as much as you humanly can will help you release false fears. Wherever you decide you will focus your emotions on, your results will be painted and created in that direction. The quicker you can shift your focus, the better you will see better results. It takes practice. Experiment for yourself so you can release yourself from the chains of man-made emotions.

This pivots us towards the topic of success, the opposite of fear. Success is uniquely defined by each person. When I contemplated this topic after many fear responses, I used an active writing conversation to work through it. I'm including the journal entry here to help you see how you can dialogue with yourself about your own idea of success.

What does success mean?

Success could be a perspective. It could be a motive. It could be a driving point.

But what is driving you?

What drives your success is what is driving the core of you.

Are you driving you?

Who is at the wheel?

Or better yet, what is driving your wheel?

Is it the need for more money, the need to get ahead, the need to fill a void, the need to find certainty, the need for approval, the need to find comfort, the need to be a part of something, or the need to feel special?

What is success then?

Success, in my eyes, is a decision you make on the outcome you want to FEEL in life. You have voices in your head that say "go to school, get a job, and you will be happy."

What is happiness then?

The word happy is a feeling. Showing pleasure or contentment. Is that what success is?

Then if success was happiness then why are so many successful business men and women live in a quiet state of sorrow?

So success must be misaligned in our society then by definition.

Why do people suddenly become inspired to live a life of pure happiness when they are faced with a terminal illness. Why do people find joy in their life when their life is about to end? Why are the old wise and the young not? Why do people see the beauty of life when they experience the birth of a child to then forget about that joy soon after they get into a routine?

The real question is.... What is your happiness?

When all that you are and all that you have may not be there tomorrow, what would be your happiness?

To me, happiness is NOW. Happiness is seeing the beauty in this experience we call life and all that we are presently intertwined in.

I used to be told that I carried a great sorrow within me. That may have been true at the time because I lost what my success was, I lost my meaning of happiness.

Your job does not define you. Your income does not define you. Your illness does not define you. Your circumstances do not define you. You define you and your happiness. Your success.

And when you search for it, it will be there. You need to feel your happiness one day, one moment, one experience at a time till it becomes so clear that you realize it's been there all along.

So, tell me then.... What is your true happiness? Your true success definition.

Chapter 10

Gratitude Simplified

We all know that in every situation we should be grateful for what we do have. Life. Sustenance. Running water. Shelter, income, or family. But it can be difficult to find something to be grateful for in a time of despair or heartbreak. Time is needed for you to come to the center of the situation and feel the power in the lesson that is presenting itself; a reflection of your own emotional state. This is what we call fine-tuning the heart. The heart is a simple but complex energy. It is a separate energy that vibrates from the rest of you. But without your heart... you would not be here. Your gratitude or appreciation must come from your heart, not your mind. Although the practice of listing things to be grateful for is helpful, it doesn't always help you get to the core feeling within your heart. Your heart is tuned into your center and knows the simplified version of everything you overcomplicate with your mind. Your emotions could be seen as an argument between mind and heart. You 'know" what needs to be done or not done but your mind (thoughts about priorities, situations, other people, work, etc) gets in the way. We then end up off our center once again in a windstorm of confusion and thoughts of scarcity.

How do you simplify the heart process?

By asking yourself what does my heart desire the most. Quickly write down what the five most important things are to you and then ask if each one is what your heart desires most. I find that most people don't even mention specifics, but general feelings that they can describe. That's when you know you are getting closer to your heart's desire. Your heart will never give you a negative emotion about a thought. If you have a negative emotion then you have stepped away from your heart's desire. If you feel a state of calm, relief, contentment, and bliss then you're beginning to feel your heart's desire, your simplified way of gratitude.

SIMPLE... life is very simple, and your heart bears witness to the simplicity of nature and its cycles. Each physical person has their own cycle that tends to create the rhythm of its physical world around them. The ebb and flow of every moment is like a heartbeat, inhalation, and exhalation. The trees dance in the wind, the rain taps its own song, the ocean waves breathe in and out as the sand dances with it. Everything in life is in a state of balance. When a hole or footprint is created in the sand, water fills the space faster than you dug or walked. When you can quiet your thoughts of negative emotions, ideas, situations, and so on; you will begin to use your intentional focus, or your will, to feel your heart's desire in every moment. Your heart FILLS the spaces just as the water and sand at the beach. Use your will as your own focus intention on what matters the most to your heart. Your heart is in the moment and only in the moment.

Your heart knows the way and you must learn to follow it. It is another way of describing following your intuition.

By following your heart, you can move from a state of lack to manifesting in physical form. This is a process that will take time depending on how far down the rabbit hole of ideas of lack and scarcity. But don't beat yourself up for where you are or try to justify with yourself why you are where you are. That only keeps you further from the heart. This is where getting to know your spiritual assets can help you adapt to enlightened thought processes, debunking thoughts that weren't yours to begin with, and verbalizing your emotions to connect back to your heart's desire. This creates your new proprietary logic that is solely based on your core and heart center. Thinking is a great tool to start off with, as we need to know where we are without pointing fingers or justifying why. Then we move into the heart, feeling your emotions and asking if this is what my heart truly wants. You can word it any way that feels best to you but know that you're asking, "How does my core feel about this?" Start with something easy that you love dearly (children, animals, nature, hiking, etc) and feel into the moment with it until you can describe it in words for yourself. Create a picture in your mind (imagination) and focus on it (will) until it feels completely normal to feel that way every day. This will help you detect when you're off your heart center and dancing in the mind again. This is an easy process that shouldn't be something that you need to force. Nothing from the heart or your spirit is forced. It's a gentle process that will teach you how to be easy with yourself. If something requires force then it will feel like your trying to swim against the current, your response should be to create space and flow with your heart. It's about your own balance within yourself. A rhythm that is unique to you and flows easily from the heart. Your manifestations will match your connection to the heart. This means your immediate manifestations will be how the next person interacts with you or the next thing you happen to stumble across. The red road in Native American culture is following the spiritual life guided by your heart, using compassion as your compass. It will never steer you wrong. It is trusting your process on this journey, to know how to empower yourself, and grow to a new level each day.

Chapter 11

Balance

Everyone seeks balance even if they cannot verbalize it at first. Work life, family life, social life, vacation life; these are all viewed as parts of your life that need to be balanced in their own separate sphere. This separation leads us to the frantic life of a person who thinks they have absolutely no time to do anything and just gives up altogether, allowing one segment of their life to take over everything else, drowning in the rat race we call "the struggle." Balance then begins to seem like a task in itself. New parents are struggling to find some kind of balance in an always changing routine of an infant; a student is struggling to find balance with school after returning from summer vacation; and a retiree is struggling to find balance in their newly found freedom from the forty-year rat race. The word struggle is placed in front of the act of finding balance so often that it is now a true manifestation of a struggle to have it. But what if you change the dialog within the words? It begins to change the feeling that comes out of the statement. For example: The first-time parents found balance as their infant progressed in their healthy routine, or the student found balance quickly due to excitement coming back from summer vacation, or the new retiree found a fun balance quickly as he filled his time with activities he always enjoyed. Changing the dialog within the context of the idea makes a world of a difference in terms of your feelings because it paints a different picture. It is a pleasant expectation and not one that is seen as a struggle from the perspective of mass consciousness.

We already know that all words have massive meaning behind them which you then internalize. This is where we would benefit the most from learning to create with intention. Understanding your own inner dialog about ideas and situations is a key component to creating and living with intention. Every situation is perspective and not descriptive. When you feel the situation happened to you will always approach things from the stance of victimhood and never from the heart. Manifestation in physical form is always formed from your feelings about any topic. If you choose to feel from the victim state than that is what you will feel over and over again until you take a hard look at your inner dialog. When you change the words attached to a situation you create new linked emotions, high vibrations, and a more relatable picture in your mind. Step-by-step the outer situation will begin to mimic the inner dialog as long as you believe that is so. We will tap into this in a later chapter but for now, start with becoming aware of the feelings you hold behind the inner dialog inside.

Knowing where you are is a large part of it. Even though time is moving, and every moment is quickly moved into the past, your understanding of your state of being (vibration) will help you identify where you are and where you would like to be next.

I say NEXT because you will never get to your final destination – the destination will always change because life in the physical dimension is about the process. Each goal we reach leads us to another, and another, and so on. What people of the masses believe is that your career or education is the beginning of your final destination, while others believe retirement is the destination. If your focus is so far off into a future that is forever changing and moving, then your manifestations in the physical will remain in the future state. What you "DO" for work or what your goals are is NOT who you are or where you are going. What you do in life can only be identified as a result of how you feel every day. Granted you will have days or moments that you feel off, but the majority of the time you should be centered on feelings that you identify as what feels good. Intention moves quicker into manifestation if you lead with how you feel most of the time while changing that inner dialog with what feels better. Your TRUE IDENTITY is not your job title, degree, relationships, or social status.... it is how you feel each day and how you maneuver those feelings while interacting with other people. Your true identity is your.... BALANCE!

Balance is something that can easily manifest if you center back to everything we have been talking about so far; be easy with yourself, give yourself permission to find your true nature, acknowledge and move forward with your feelings, and change the dialog in your mind to what feels better. Once you begin to feel good more often, your mind starts to compartmentalize what is important to you, what makes sense, what you should start to question, and what's your own unique truth about your life. Your balance will begin when you pay less attention to other opinions, conversations, and actions and you are truly comfortable with yourself. You should understand by now that this is their journey, not yours to interject into. Balance is knowing when to let go of your idea of control on others and focus on what you can control.... only YOU. If your mind goes "but, but, but...." remember that it is your mind talking and not your spirit. Your spirit immediately says "FINALLY" while your conditioned mind has excuses to not relinquish its tight grip on a false reality.

At first, you may hate this idea. You may laugh at it. You may roll your eyes and play with all the recurring feelings until you hit a wall again. Either way, there will be a part of you that desires to feel centered and balanced; and through that one desire you will begin to see your walls coming down. Start to detach yourself from what some material things or relationships make you feel and focus on what is important to the center of you. Focus on fun, joy, bliss, happiness, and most of all... love.

Chapter 12

Belief and Faith

$\mathcal{B}$elief and faith have different meanings. For our purposes we will identify belief as a conditioned pattern of thought that has created your own logic; while faith is learning to trust without needing an explanation to why or how. Each person has their own beliefs and faith in whatever they acknowledge as a higher power or centered energy force. Belief can usually be bolstered with evidence and facts until you accept it as a truth to you. Each organized religion has a faith and each person has their own beliefs that determine their level of faith. This is where we conclude that it is your own experience that determines if it moves from a belief to faith.

Now let's turn your attention back to you and your own beliefs. Believing in yourself is the first step in creating your manifesting world consciously. "Believe in yourself" seems like a filler when someone doesn't understand how someone can feel so terrified to take action on something. But we are going to take a much closer look at YOU than you ever thought possible. Depending on where you currently are, you have a set of beliefs that determine how you look at the world, how your inner dialog operates, and how you feel from day-to-day. It is experience-based. Meaning; what you have experienced to date is what you have been conditioned to believe is right and wrong; good and bad. While you start to seek balance in your world, your world will reflect back to you what you believe is true. Call it the law of attraction or whatever you want, but the truth is that your beliefs can hold you in a holding pattern for as long as you allow them to keep playing with your mind. Believing in yourself (your perception of your ability to be or have anything in this lifetime) is your first step into having faith in yourself.

Faith is your ability to have confidence in your job within the creation process of manifestation. All you are responsible for is remembering your center. The center you slowly forgot as you woke up in this human life. Children understand so much more than we as adults could ever comprehend about the "truth" of life. Allow them to be themselves and watch them as they bloom into the spirits they desired to be before they stepped forward. Your faith is more than what you deem as your higher power.... your faith is your moment to moment feeling of complete joy and love for everything you come into contact within this lifetime; trusting your journey. Keep in mind that a person who has a strong "faith" has a knowing that where the dark is there will always be light that can flood the room faster than a light switch on a wall turning on. It's a complete letting go and relaxing into the unknown without expectation of a certain path; it's releasing the how and allowing your feeling of the outcome to manifest for the good. Your beliefs, your experience-based ideas, will keep your faith from growing if you do not allow yourself to acknowledge your feelings from moment to moment. Your feelings will help you identify if you are experiencing faith (spirit guided) or a belief (conditioned ideas and experiences). Again, your inner dialog will play a key role in helping you know if something has moved from a belief to complete faith.

When you start to move from having ideas about a topic to having faith, the emotions of it become clearer. We are born to create the world around us and with a growing faith within yourself you will see the manifestations in physical form. Time will feel like it slows down and speeds up when you desire it to. You naturally let go of the how and allow the universe to fill in the spaces of the how while you savor the experience. When something "bad" happens, remember that it is a perceived belief that is moving into a balanced state like how a pendulum swings. It shows you what is out of balance. Balance is then experienced, and you start to let go of what no longer serves you in this ever-growing state. Please understand that if you have a very strong desire that is coming from anywhere else besides emotions of love and joy then time needs to elapse for your belief to move into a faith for the desired outcome. You may be putting too many specifics on the path and the beliefs or emotions behind it are keeping you in a holding pattern. This is very common in our overthinking world now, which is why we now have some people deciding that the law of attraction does not work. Do not waste any time trying to pick apart how you came to these limiting beliefs, instead allow your feelings to move from the ideas of lack to expansion and bliss. You will know you have started to switch it when inspiration strikes that feels exciting and uplifting.

Chapter 13

Determining Goals or Focus Points

Now to the old topic of goals. This is an old way of doing things. As I became a "thinker" and paralyzed myself in lists of goals and desires... it made me feel like I was on a sinking ship with no rescue boat in sight. That being said I am NOT a fan of overthinking goals and making long lists of wants if you're completely stuck in a holding pattern. Some people can take one goal and hold onto it like a dog on a bone. Some people, like myself, choose understanding more about life, spirit, and the inner workings of the universe over a goal for a new car. I was NEVER happy reporting to my mentors my biggest goal because it made me feel I could never reach it. I would cry out in desperation because my results kept getting worse instead of better. That was when I knew that goal setting was NOT my cup of tea. When I was in my early 20's my life began to fall apart. I turned to drugs and alcohol in hopes it would fill the void I felt so deep inside. The day I tried to take my life my one-year-old rescue dog sat at my feet and begged me to smile, to laugh, and to stop what I was doing. I looked into the eyes of the one I chose to be my pal for life and made another choice... "I will try for you". The reason for telling you about my experience is to underline the importance of CHOICE! Goals need a new understanding... it's a choice, a leaping off point, a no-turning-back decision, something you feel deep within yourself even if you haven't felt much up to that point. People have experiences like this all the time. Mine was linked with my dog because animals were ALWAYS my safe place; the best way my spirit could reach me. I could sit in the grass all day with my dog as a child and feel completely free and loved.

It's the feelings that help you see through the mind and into the heart.

Goals are FOCUS POINTS not destinations. They are star stickers you get as a child for potty training or getting a good grade on your report card. Goals have a unique meaning to you based upon your beliefs. If you came from a competitive upbringing than you may thrive off of goals and tasks, while others who were raised and condemned for not reaching a goal will have a negative belief behind goals. Focus points are based on feelings, then put into words to make a "goal". If you continue to ignore your feelings, then the cycles will remain the same till you make a new choice to look at them. Your focus points should be the feelings that matter the most to you: feelings like love, comfort, freedom, and joy. Then allow the universe or your higher power to fill in the journey for you. You are solely responsible for YOU and your own inner dialog. ASKING yourself and the invisible forces around you (even if you don't know what the invisible forces are) for help will allow the universe to help you along the way. We made a choice to be here. We made a choice to wake up. We made a choice to keep moving forward. We make the choice to relive a cycle or break it. You can demand it in your mind to break a cycle but if you are not in line with your feelings on that topic, meaning aligned with your heart, then it will continue to repeat.

You will need to identify if an idea or focus point you are reaching for is your idea or someone else's. We are distracted by social media and conversations alike that put thoughts in your mind of what happiness or success is by the masses. If you are unsure if your focus point is your idea, then just ask that question inside. Relax, and then let it go. Sit back and enjoy the show as the universe responds. Start to notice how the world answers your question in conversations, chance meetings, a phone call, or something that catches your eye. Start to trust in the letting go process and become more aware of the now. You may not be fully ready yet to heal from everything at once; remember it's a journey. Time will begin to slow down and your center will start to shine through. Your focus points should be that of obtaining a feeling that feels better than where you are right now. A feeling that you want to achieve each and every day. The result will show itself in your everyday life. In the beginning, all I could focus on was feeling happy each moment possible. Because if I didn't focus on that, my surroundings reflected my inner frustration and anguish. I would fight with my spouse or get upset over the smallest task not going right. Once you identify your focus point and reach for it as often as you can... you will see the manifestations around you as you change that belief into faith.

It's never really been about goals then, has it? The younger generations intuitively sense that happiness is not obtained by driving the faster car or having the biggest house. They feel and know it... we just forgot it. Life becomes this beautiful dance between the physical world, your mind, and your spirit. Yes, money can be a focus point but make sure the feeling comes from a focus point that feels good and doesn't have a laundry list of bad stories or attachments to them. Start small with feelings of freedom or happiness and allow the world to dance with you as you come to clarity on what really matters to you. You should see the patterns now. This has never been rocket science but yet there are thousands of marketing strategies out there that will tell you how to be a millionaire or success magnet when the average toddler can tell you what is most important in life. We just FORGOT! Know that all you ever NEED is your own willingness to take a look at your inner dialog, feelings, and future worry in order to get yourself back into balance with this life. Be humble, be the cup that is empty and willing to fill it with what feels true, be curious about every moment, and STOP TAKING THINGS PERSONALLY. Everyone you know and love is going through the same thing in their own unique way. Be still and hold a space for yourself and loved ones to expand into what is uniquely yours to create in this reality.

Chapter 14

Holding Space For What's To Come

Holding a space for the universe to fill in the gaps for what's to come will test your faith on a different level. Trusting that everything will always work out for your highest good is a new skill that creates a humble and calm manner. Being relaxed helps you remain neutral during the here and now, whether it's good or bad. Being in the present moment as much as possible will help you release your tight grip on your future predictions that may or may not be of the heart's desire. Being humble is having the gracious ability and understanding that "you don't know what you don't know." All you need to do is ASK for what it is your heart desires and then let it go, holding the infinite space for it to flow into your physical reality. If you keep asking over and over again then you are not holding a space or being in the moment. You are pushing it further and further into the future when the answer is right here, right now. The feelings you feel right away give you the feedback of your connection to the truth (it feels good) or the ego of it (the fear-based creation of reality). This is why meditation is a skill taught by many

Guru's before they will teach spiritual knowledge. One must learn to quiet the mind, feel the heart, feel the pulse of the world, feel the spaces within the spaces, and become neutral. Just think how annoying it is for someone to continually tell you to calm down when you're in a state of fight or flight.... it's just not going to happen. The guru's needed to put people through a process that would demonstrate how you operate best after quieting your mind, feeling the energy that flows all around us, and becoming that energy. When you practice quieting your mind you will begin to dream, imagine, and breathe easier. Things that used to make you frantic don't seem as important anymore. In other words, you are practicing holding a space for what's to come to you.

Visualizing what you desire is a great tool in the asking process. It creates a bookmark in your mind to recall feelings or vibrations of what that image in your mind equals. The language of the universe has never been one of dialects, instead it is all about vibrations and how those interpret to you. It's about using your feelings as your compass and moving from one focus point to another. That's why life is FUN! Use your perception and see this physical life as a journey, a playground, and experiment each day on how you can make the next day even better! The masses are drowning in a perception problem. Everyone else's perception dictates your own. If ideas do not feel good... don't give them any more of your attention. PERIOD! I was once told by an emotional empath that "you seem to be emotionless at times". As I burst out in laughter I responded with "I don't engage in conversations or situations that do not feel good or have someone in the middle that cannot see beyond the problem." You see, you do not need to engage in acts with others that do not serve the parties involved for the best. It's a vicious cycle of vibrations being interpreted in a dark light rather than for what they are. SO do not engage. You can listen and be a helping hand in a solution but do not get yourself involved in the vibrational drama of the egos. Again, if it does not feel good then you are not holding a space for things to manifest as you have been intending. Instead, you add a mixture of vibrations that do not serve your highest intention for good. Using situations like this as feedback for your own vibrational state at the moment is also very helpful in knowing how you can detach yourself from others' reactions. Love this feedback even if it feels judgmental from other parties because each moment is a teachable moment towards your growth.

Epictetus stated, "you have two ears and one mouth so that we can listen twice as much as we speak." The more you speak on topics the less you are listening from within. The more you speak the less interpreting you can do vibrationally in your mind consciously. Learning when to talk and when to listen is a wonderful tool. When was the last time you heard the trees sing as the wind dances through its leaves? When was the last time you heard the rain's rhythmic beat as it dances off your roof? The more you speak the more you justify your lack of results. BE still. Be neutral. It isn't wrong to speak but learning when to listen will help you in mediation, being in the present moment, and holding that space for what's to come. It creates a new level of appreciation for this physical realm we live in. Our world is thriving no matter what the media says. Appreciation is choosing to see the love, joy, and beauty all around. It doesn't mean you must go out today and become a tree hugger. Just start with appreciating where you are right here right now. Appreciation will stop your mind from taking over and creating a laundry list of things to do and worry about.

What can you control? Only YOU right here right now! Understand that there is no hurry to get anywhere and stay open to what's coming.

Chapter 15

The Art of Detachment

Detaching ourselves from certain thoughts, behaviors, actions, and control is a skill that is not taught in school. Babies naturally know what they have control over until someone else decides that they need to learn to control something else beyond them to keep someone else happy. Babies have no thoughts associated with the self or egos attached to their process of thinking.

We have established so far that the only thing you have control over is YOU. How you think, behave, respond, and speak. That is what you control. Then that would mean that everything you have experienced in your life so far is based solely on what you have attached yourself to. Attached to ideas and thoughts that keep clouding your mind and judgment of what to do or not to do. The art of detachment is knowing what you have control over within the creation process. If you only control you then you should keep your thoughts to yourself until you're ready to detach from them. Nothing good in history has come from attachment. It has always been a fight over power, land, people, etc. The human species thinks it can control things that are way beyond its physical limits. That then creates FEAR.

So how do you learn to detach yourself from things you cannot control? It is a very simple concept that relaxed my mind within seconds. The concept is acknowledging that everything is impermanent! Everything in our lives is in a constant state of movement and because of that nothing belongs to anyone besides the energy source it came from. Your house does not belong to you or even the bank. You have seen how some people react after a house fire. Some people are completely devastated over the "stuff" they lost in a fire while another family may be relieved because their entire family made it out together. It's not about the "stuff"! When you realize the parts of you that matter the most, you will see it isn't stuff! It's the energy from family, love, your connections to your community and friends. Because deep down, you know the land you purchased with a deed doesn't really belong to you... it belongs to its original energy source (to whomever or whatever you deem is that source). Don't get me wrong, it's nice to have stuff, drive the cars you want, buy a house you want, or go and travel the world as you wish. We are physical beings that came here to live a physical life and we have physical things that add to the reality we choose to live. But it's stuff! Once you detach yourself from the idea that this is mine and that is his or hers, then you will start to see the core of it.... it brings you enjoyment, love, experience, and FUN!

Our attachment to living, and all the concerns for physical survival which that entails, then fosters deep fears that feed our ego's feelings of greed, lack, and jealousy. When you begin to see through the fear of losing something you will see the love and beauty behind it. The reason why you have a nice house or car is linked to your core needs which ultimately equal out to a feeling. Identify the feeling you are trying to attain through the acquisition of the physical item and may find you don't actually *need* the item all; rather, you will be able to simply enjoy it because the attainment ADDS to your already loving experience. See the difference?

Be open and patient with yourself. We live an objective life with free will to accompany it. It's about living NOW and living with your heart open. Every corner you take is another opportunity to drop the chains of attachment from the ego and be one with your center. Now don't be so serious all the time either! A sense of humor is an important key to this life. Humor helps you break down barriers of attachment and make light of how your ego chatters in your mind about why this is so important. If the heart of it isn't love, then it's your ego talking. If you are afraid of what others will think of your new way of being, then you are attached to how they make you feel over the value of your own inner perspective. Again, everything is impermanent! Check in with yourself often to see what you are focusing on in the moment. If you feel anything BUT serenity then you are attached to an idea, person, or situation that no longer serves you. Your ego HATES change, and it will do anything to keep you from not needing it anymore. In fact, the more you think the more the ego keeps you in a prison... you. Ask yourself where is my energy going today? Where do you feel it in your body? This helps keep you grounded and in your body. Too many people do not take the time to know where their energy is focused at any given moment thus leading them to be outside of their body and not in the here and now. The movement and change you are seeking is an energy force inside you that needs to be awakened. Too many distractions in today's world have your ego scrolling through social media just to buy some time to find the next things to panic about, compare, or be jealous over. The ego is an all-consuming energy that is created by your own thinking. Be open and patient with yourself. Notice your actions and where it's leading you. Notice where you can start to detach and what needs more work.

Worry equals a negative wish! I bet what you are so worried about is something out of your control or needs more time for an answer. Remember you are not here to FIX anyone. No one is broken! No one needs fixing or mending. Most people just need help finding their center and what speaks uniquely to them. Focus more on where you are putting your energy and less on worrying about things you cannot control. Do things that make you happy. Things won't change unless you detach yourself from the outcome you think may or may not happen. You are here to remember YOU and not to complete anything or anyone else. There is no hard struggle besides the one you put on yourself. There is no mission. There is only a journey to rediscovering who you are at the core and all the good that can flourish from it. A successful relationship in all categories is when two complete people come together as completes which in turn makes an even larger complete. It's not your half and my half... it's two complete pies coming together to make one larger one. Do not worry, do not start the excuse list. Just find and be you fully. Your journey started long before the day you were conceived. Everything that you have experienced to this date has prepared you to see the clarity you have been asking for, or even screaming for. Make the room for it now by the art of detachment. I love to use the idea of beta testing everything. Everything is an experiment to me. This attitude takes the pressure off my back and I can move forward without attaching myself to inauthentic ideas or the voices of others. Since everything is impermanent, why should we worry so much when we came here to fully embrace the love and support that is always here for us? You answer that question for yourself.

Chapter 16

Remembering and Awakening

As you begin to consciously make connections with your core, notice when the ego steps in. Living from the heart; you are helping more than yourself. You are helping all your loved ones and benefiting mass consciousness. Heart-centered living affects generational lines both past, present, and future in a positive manner.

Remembering and awakening your core is learning how to love yourself unconditionally. In loving yourself unconditionally you are adding love to all time, space, and realities. So, it is an honor to remember yourself because it has such a strong benefit for everyone, not just yourself. That in itself should help you with thoughts of selfishness. You are never alone in this process and our goal in life is to remember the unconditional love we knew was here for us all along. Be easy with yourself. Honor your core, your heart's desires, and each breath you take. There is no need to tell anyone what they need or want, you only need to work on your own connection with your core. This is a healing process that is unique to you. Self-love will not only honor your core but will help you heal in an orderly fashion that is specific to you. Your heart may need to heal first before you can learn to speak your truth or vice versa. Everyone has a unique pattern of coming together to their own truth of who they are designed to be.

Find your still point in the silence.

Do not allow yourself to get overwhelmed and settle back into the rat race of life. That will only remind you of your ego taking control again. Once your intentions are known to the universe you cannot stop the process from unfolding. That is why this is a journey. You can take many turns, go off-road, or drive on the highway for a bit. Either way, the road trip always has the best memories. Know that remembering and awakening is a process of learning to think consciously; to make choices that serve your highest and best, and then learning to let the thinking go completely and allow the universe to fill in the blanks while you focus on being in the here and now. Then it's time to focus on the space between the spaces, the love in everything you see and feel. The space between the spaces? It's the stillness you feel when you quiet your mind long enough so you can feel your surroundings without opening your eyes. You sense the energy pulsing around you till you no longer can tell your head from your feet. The unconditional love pluses in those spaces. This is when you remember what it feels like to BE without thinking.

Chapter 17

Separating Mind and Heart

Now we are at a turning point, one that you will begin to feel just before you turn the corner and see a new horizon. We have taught you to think, to use your mind in a manner that will separate your ego from the soft nudges of your heart. It takes practice, dedication to love yourself unconditionally, to love everyone for where they are on their journey and BE the pure light you are; energy dancing in a physical world. Your outer world should not affect your inner world. But the outer world is a reflection of all inner worlds.

Thinking is where western society believes the answers are. That we must be in a constant state of thinking and doing. This may have started with Descartes, a western philosopher who stated, "I Think therefore I am". But he didn't quite penetrate the mind as far as some other seekers. Buddha went beyond the mind, into the depths of the stillness, and to a point to wait for further instructions from the soul. But the Buddha also realized that one must learn to live with both the mind and spirit in a non-dualistic manner.

It is not so much separating the mind from the heart but learning to live consciously with both. Knowing when you are leading with the mind (asleep at the wheel) or leading with your heart (awakening). It's a process of feeling more and speaking less. Language is debilitating as the ego of each individual can react to words differently. The prison you believe you are living in is your own mind, ego, and belief structures. As you walk forward on your journey you will begin to see the illusion of this life, also known as Maya, illusion of the self. The mask you wear each day is the body you walk in. Separating yourself from the mask allows you to see that the outer world should not affect your inner world. The more curious you become of the stillness that moves with you, the more the illusion will fall away. To live with both the mind and your spirit you must recognize this life is a gift, something to treasure because the answers are always in the stillness of your consciousness.

Life is not about getting to the top of the mountain. The destination IS the journey. It is what the heart craves. Live with an evolving faith; learning that leaping into the unknown in the depths of your heart will yield you an experience of BEING. Feel each step along the way and dance with the duality of it. Releasing your resistance to all that is unknown. Resistance is feeding your ego with thinking. Painting pictures of what the unknown could really be like. Instead, feeling from your heart, there is no resistance but a welcoming to the duality of it all. How do you know if you're awake if you haven't fallen asleep? Sometimes we must slip from our awakened state to feel the duality. Honor yourself in the fact that we must learn to live with both the mind and spirit. In Asian Monk traditions it is said that "the mind is a wonderful servant but a terrible master." This should illustrate to you what your core desires to lead with. Thinking is a great tool when it is in harmony with the heart. If your mind is locked into your physical senses, it will create more for the ego to fear. This journey is like a blooming flower, or lotus as the center is the jewel to life. Know yourself better in your stillness than your words can describe. That is the center of you.

Chapter 18

The Truth of it All

Our society is always seeking the truth. As you can begin to see the horizon you can taste the fruit of the spirit. You are here to evolve into a heightened state of love and joy. To feel the fruits of your own spirit and walk the outer world with a spiraling inner world of love and joy. You may find others who run from your very presence because their ego can see your inner world. Others will gravitate towards you as they begin their process of awakening in and out of a deep slumber of illusion. Dance with the duality of your life as your manifestations are created from your inner world. If you do not like the outer world you see, your focus must turn to your own inner world. Do not participate in actions that separate you from your spirit. In today's world, there is a war against everything; hunger, disease, terrorism, etc. The wars are a reflection of what is going on inside each person's inner world. One by one, each person will find themselves at a crossroad; do they follow the masses or choose to walk out of the dark cave and face the light? The light might blind you at first but give yourself time to adjust and the view will come in clearer.

Albert Einstein was a remarkable man. He penetrated deep beyond the mind to find the transcendental force that pulses through all consciousness: liberation of the self from mind and ego. He intellectualized the act of transcendental meditation, finding the stillness with the spaces of our center. He found what he called "pure being", a form of an effortless and natural way of our being. It takes time, years even, but the intentions you form with your heart will yield you to experiences that will feed your spirit instead of the ego. To awaken, you must acknowledge that you are asleep; and we fall asleep at the wheel of life time and time again to have the experience of remembering that coming home feeling; that pure feeling of being without attachment or desire.

What are we describing here? There is a poem by John Godfrey Saxe called "Blind Men and the Elephant", where he describes the very thing we are talking about. Six blind men stand at a different part of the elephant's body and each declares that their section is the totality of what an elephant is. The blind man standing at the elephant's stomach describes the animal as a wall. The second blind man stands at the elephant's tusk, declaring the animal a spear. The third blind man stands at the elephant's trunk while saying the animal is like a snake. The fourth blind man stands at the elephant's leg, feeling it and deeming the animal like a tree. The fifth blind man approaches the elephant's ear, describing the elephant is like a fan. The final blind man touches the tail of the elephant and then declares the animal is a rope. The point? Everything is like the elephant and the blind men. Everyone is explaining different parts of the same thing. Mythology, theology, philosophy, spiritualism, etc.... they are all describing parts of the same thing stating their conclusion is what is accurate. The only way you can find out the truth is if you do the work and go within.

We all want answers. We all want to KNOW what's in the unknown. But understand that desiring for the truth, in itself, is an act from the ego. To want to be more spiritual, more evolved, more enlightened IS acting from the ego and not the heart. That is why Einstein called this process one that is effortless and natural. There are many names for this process Einstein studied and published. There are many techniques but understand that it requires the working of both the mind and spirit to transcend into pure being. Focus and willingness of the mind will allow you to drop the resistance to reach the heart or spirit. Each person is unique in their own journey to pure being, pure love, and pure enjoyment. Know that you are never alone on this journey. Get to know yourself through thinking, then drop it ALL, allowing your mind to transcend into the pureness that is spiraling inside. Your mind tries to keep you busy doing actions, but it is important to feel from your center, inner world, and awaken your truth. It is something no one can touch or tamper with, it is unique to you and only felt from within. As you feel your inner world, your outer world will reflect that which is from within. That in itself should spark your mind to want to feel from the heart.

You are here to evolve into pure love. Just imagine how your world would change if you began to walk away from the masses and be warmed by the light of the unknown.

Keep your ego in check and love the beautiful life of duality and unfoldment. Follow your curiosity. Follow your heart. Listen more from within and feel for the soft nudges that have always been there. You're not broken, you do not need to be fixed, and it is time to come back around to this... you have never been disconnected. You have only been asleep at the wheel as your heart waits patiently for the moment you can awaken, feel the clarity, and then do it over and over again. Your map is your own discovery of mind and spirit. **Know that the mind is a wonderful tool but your spirit, your heart, your center is the MASTER.**

Chapter 19

Putting it Together

This process gives you a starting point but the map to your unfoldment will be unique to you. Are you ready to see what it looks like? We've given you the steps to guide you along your journey, to help you refocus when needed, and give you the encouragement to listen to your heart. Your map will allow you to dismantle the ego so you can easily listen and feel your true nature, which means that the steps you take will be yours, and yours alone.

Here's how to start:

1: **Why am I here?** Because you KNOW there is more to life than what you see. You're not disconnected; you are asleep at the wheel. In fact, you have accepted your reality as your ego as experienced it. The only control you have is to relinquish the filters in your mind, dismantling the ego that holds tight to this physical reality. This is the first step of realizing you may not know who you really are. This may be scary. You must admit now you have been asleep.

3: **Ask yourself the right questions:**

What does this mean to me?

What was the prominent feeling in this situation?

What would I want to feel instead?

These questions help you understand where you are and where your conditioned mind is taking you. From here you begin to compartmentalize what is truly from the heart and what stems from conditioned circumstance. If you tend to seek out pleasure to avoid pain, focus on what others think of you, or seek out distractions or other stimuli because you cannot be fulfilled without it... then you have to recognize you're asleep. Realizing these behaviors feed your ego to only keep you asleep is part of this process. Don't label them, just let them be, allow them to fall away and be ok with filling the spaces with silence holding a space for your true self to come through. Don't bury your head in the sand by seeing your patterns and not be willing to let them go. You must be willing to let go of the old patterns, the structure that has been built to keep you DOING and not BEING. You are limitless! Some part of you knows this is true.

3: **Purpose**: Pondering your purpose examines what you have done to date. It is not placed on the map to make you reconsider everything in your past; but instead, to do a life review. To look at what you have done that makes your heart sing, to find those moments when your ego wasn't the controlling factor. You did things a certain way because it was guided to you without you knowing it. Hence why you lost track of time or stood up for yourself without realizing why. It's a discovery process that will help you in dismantling what everyone else wants for you vs what YOU feel is right.

4: **Vision:** Feel from your heart and KNOW what your core values are. What does your gut tell you is important to you? Those are the soft nudges through the cracks of the ego to help you find your way back to your heart. Use your mind and put aside all that you know and open the flood gates to imagine the "what if..." life without limitations. Exercise your mind into a new perspective, one that is full of the wellbeing and peace you desire. This is where things like vision boarding, freewriting, and art booking can be helpful.

5: **Decision:** This is you learning to say NO to what no longer serves you and YES to your inner self, your spirit, your heart. Now, we aren't telling you to quit your job or jump into a boat to float across the sea, but we are saying to give yourself permission to feel into the unknown. You must question everything and bring everything to the forefront of your mind that you think you know. Your questioning alone will create the change you're looking for. Go beyond your questioning and go into your feelings. Feel for the sticky points and then feel for the love, it will never steer you wrong. Keep your mind away from what you think is your current reality and feel from your heart as you make decisions. Things should excite you with a healthy amount of fear. Go with your gut and don't allow the fear to block you.

6: **Handling the Blocks:** If you feel something is blocking you, you're right. If you feel there is a gate that you must open;

you're right. The blocks, gates, or any images that you feel are in your way exist in your mind only. The conditioned mind holds tightly to paradigms that have constructed the illusion of self. The ego is the identification of the self so you must realize that the conditioned behaviors are not yours to begin with: they are something you have adopted through the guidance of society. It is now your job to drop them, question them, doubt them, and let them go one by one. Each time you drop one, you will be able to look at life and make decisions from the perspective of your heart, your true self, and less from your mind and ego.

7: **Use the Mind as a TOOL:** Thinking is a wonderful tool when it is used as a servant to the heart. Question EVERYTHING your mind brings into focus while using the spiritual assets. You were born with no preconceived perception of reality, then grew up learning everyone else's perceptions and have spent the rest of your life trying to dismantle those very perceptions that have shaped your ego to date. Some people fear that they will lose their identity in this process. Instead, know that you will gain a sense of individuality that cannot be tampered with by anyone else. The ego thrives on creating barriers, everything is either good or bad to it. Your heart is unique and will vibrate out such a uniqueness that the acknowledgment of others will no longer matter as you are completely fulfilled in any situation.

8: **The Fear, Faith, & Beliefs:** This is the test before the gates of the awakened consciousness, the heart. This is the moment when you decide to jump into the unknown but KNOW that you will float on the other side. Walking in the dark and knowing your footing is strong and safe. This is following your heart and holding your focus on the heart. If you are afraid, your mind is controlling the situation. If you have doubts, your beliefs are doubting the decision. If you have faith, you are stepping off the ledge KNOWING there is a place to land on. That is where freedom really is. It has never been about self-development or self-improvement, it has only been about dismantling the self, the ego, and recognizing the heart center.

9: **The focus point is in the silence:** The source of all being is a still point or your own personal, magical black hole, your access point to Source. It's where everything is still but yet it is still moving. It is where you focus on yourself or an object until it completely disappears in your mind. You may come face-to-face with the pain, but that's okay: the pain is the feelings you work through as you allow the candle to burn on both ends. To follow your heart, you must create focus points that are in alignment with where you are and where you want to be. The feelings are what we must focus in tandem with the inner dialog you have with yourself. This will help you identify and compartmentalize the ego and allow it to drop away.

10: **Allowing:** This is the practice of letting go of resistance. Our mind is what creates the resistance. Any feelings that do not feel good are created from the mind, the self. Notice how many headaches or stomach pains you get when you are stressed out or worried. Sometimes, your heart literally hurts. You have created so much resistance that it is affecting you on a physical level. The art of detachment and knowing what you are responsible for will help you in holding a space for your true nature to shine through. You will find your heart in the still point, the inward movement of the silence that will give you the peace you need right now to move forward. This process takes time and willingness on your part shed the old and explore what lies beyond what your mind has identified as you. The worse you feel, the more resistance; the better you feel, the less resistance.

11: **Finding what works for you**: Every thought has created our world and has created your experiences. The ego sees everything as good or bad. The ego requires a barrier at all times. This entire process is about dismantling the ego slowly, so it does not fight you at the gates of the awakened consciousness: your truth. This process of dismantling the ego has been done through techniques like transcendental meditation, chanting, ceremonies, hallucinogenic medicines, etc. The use of techniques is helpful in the dismantling process but be warned that when the techniques themselves become a desire or need to perform them then the ego has its grip on them and is trying to take you away from the gate of your truth. You WILL fall asleep at the wheel... that's part of the process. You WILL never be fully awakened all the time... that is part of this human experience. But you CAN and WILL make MASSIVE change within yourself, your environment, and ultimately your life for the positive.

12: **When in doubt, follow the heart:** At times during this process you may feel that you don't know who you are. That's because you have identified yourself with what your ego has created your entire life. This can create an inner imbalance that fosters many of the unwanted experiences in your life. Don't be afraid of what you don't know about yourself. Coming from a neutral state, a loving state, a state of an empty glass humbly waiting for the stillness to dance with you around grandfather fire, get ready to jump across the fire and transcend into the eternalness that has been available to you since the beginning of time. It's a breath away, a practiced space of holding, a channel that will make you feel nothing but everything at the same time. You will be freed of perspectives and be opened to freely find new perspectives that do not create more control from the ego. Everything transcends through you and out of you like a clear vessel. Thought is not a bad thing; it is a TOOL to use in this lifetime to distinguish the heart or soul's direction.

Key Points to Remember:

1. You don't know what you don't know.
2. Look at yourself with a new lens of perception: "I am LOVE, I am eternal, I am transcending."
3. Realize that you are wearing a mask of illusion, but we chose to wear it and play the part: it's the human experience.
4. Pure love and joy are expansive... you can and will expand with it as it's the way of the heart.
5. You can create more change in yourself and your surroundings when you act from an inner peace instead of reacting to circumstances.

Black Elk of the Lakota tribe stated in the book of *The First Peace; My Search for the better Angels* by Charles Wilson Hatfield: "The first peace, which is the most important, is that which comes from within the souls of ... (people) when they realize their relationship, their oneness with the universe and all its Powers, and when they realize that at the center of the universe, dwells ... (the Great Mystery), and that this center is really everywhere, it is within each of us. This is the real Peace, and the others are but reflections of this. The second peace is that which is made between two individuals, and the third is that which is made between two nations. But above all, you should understand that there can never be peace between nations until there is first known that true peace which is within ... (our) souls ..."

Black Elk said it profoundly, that what you are reaching for is within you. That you must go inward and find the inner stillness to make the shift to peace. It starts with the first peace, you.

This book has been an attempt to explain what is limitless, what is beyond your conditioned mind, what is in your spirit. It is timeless, boundless, all-knowing without need. Words cannot teach nor can it begin to explain an experience that can only be felt within your center, one that is profoundly unique to your nature. Seeking the right definition only allows your ego to grab toward something else it wants to control. Allow the process to unfold without effort. This is an effortless state of being found within the heart of each person. A tug and pull process of mind and heart. A focus within the mind and an allowing of the heart to take the center. It's not what you think, and it will blow your thinking away each time because the mind cannot construct what is limitless.

Life is a beautiful gift, one in which we were granted the ability to forget what we once knew, and then experience the remembering. It's a beautiful unfolding of realizing, awakening, remembering, and being who you really are NOW. Awaken from your slumber and unfold. Your map is unique. All you have to do is decide, listen, and embark on this journey of remembering. The world needs you to step forward and reignite your truth.

About the Author

Sarah Breen, LMT, CCMT, is a mother of two young boys, rescue dog mom, and loving wife who has spent her entire life rediscovering her purpose and enjoying the unique process of her journey. At the age of 20, she almost committed suicide in her attempt to see beyond where she stood physically. Like many people, she lost her connection to her inner self as a teenager through a series of life experiences that led her on an unhealthy path. Her choice to stay was in alignment with her highest intention to serve others in mind and spiritual crisis. Thus, began her spiritual journey, leading her to discover paths of spiritual and mind development.

Sarah is an Intuitive Life Coach with Mind Spirit Mapping, helping people reconnect themselves with who they really are; igniting the flame from within using the help from guides and ancestors. She guides people through pain points to freedom of the heart by connecting you with spirit. She is also an Integrative shamanic bodyworker and healer, using sound therapy, massage, and reiki to help you reconnect soul pieces while realigning energy centers for optimal healing on both physical and spiritual levels. She has and continues to study Shamanic techniques through an apprenticeship with a Shamanic mentor. Sarah reveres the ancient Shamanic traditions and does not title herself as a Shaman, instead identifying as a certified Shamanic Lightworker. She incorporates mediumship, sound healing, and the shamanic arts with permission from her guides, mentors, and ancestors to apply in her daily practice for herself and everyone she encounters. She also took her love to canines, working side by side with an animal behaviorist to help owners and pets reconnect through the heart using touch, intention, and lots of patience. Her intention is to help you heal yourself; and by healing yourself, you are helping heal the masses, and our planet.

Please visit http://www.MindSpiritMapping.com
for more information and a list of workshops to help you
on your journey.

More Earth Lodge® Books

The Teen Transformation Manual

The Comprehensive Vibrational
Healing Guide

Magical Mudras

Grounding and Clearing

Conversations with Stones

Simple and Natural Herbal Living

The Healing Properties of Flowers

Equine Herbs & Healing

Energy Healing for Animals

Palm Reading for Everyone

Natural Animal Healing

Tarot

Post Magic

Shades of Valhalla

The Warping

Song Walker

The Girls Who Could

Made in the USA
Monee, IL
03 September 2023